Singled Out

Maximizing The Single Season

Ibukun Adewusi

CCCG Publishing House

Copyright © 2024 Ibukun Adewusi

All rights reserved. No part of this book may be used or reproduced by any means, graphics, electronic, or mechanical, including photocopying, recording, taping or by any information storage retrieval system without the author's written permission except in cases of brief quotations embodied in critical articles and reviews.

Scripture quotations marked:

- NLT are taken from the New Living Translation. Copyright © 1996, 2004, 2007 by Tyndale House Foundation. Used by permission of Tyndale House Publishers, Inc., Carol Stream, Illinois 60188. All rights reserved.

- NKJV are taken from the New Kings James Version®. Copyright © 1982 by Thomas Nelson. Used by permission. All rights reserved.

- AMP are taken from the Amplified Version. Copyright © 2015 by The Lockman Foundation, La Habra, CA 90631. All rights reserved.

- TPT are taken from The Passion Translation®. Copyright © 2017, 2018, 2020 by Passion & Fire Ministries, Inc. Used by permission. All rights reserved. ThePassionTranslation.com.

- CEV are taken from Contemporary English Version (CEV)® © 1995 by American Bible Society. Used by permission. All rights reserved.

Author: Ibukun Adewusi

ISBN: 978-1-989099-56-8 (hardcover)

ISBN: 978-1-989099-57-5 (ebook)

First Printing 2024

Contents

Dedication	IV
Introduction	V
Section I	1
1. The Essence of Being Singled Out	2
Section II	10
2. Build an Intimate Relationship with God	11
3. Deal With Any Trauma	24
4. Discover and Understand Your Design	41
5. Discover and Run With Your Vision	59
6. Build Your Character	70
7. Visualize Your Desired Future	78
Epilogue	83
A Sinner's Prayer	85
Contact the Author	87
About the Author	89
Additional References	91

Dedication

To the Holy Spirit (H.S), thank You for being my Helper. You saw me through my single season and I'm extremely grateful for riding with me through that season. Thank you for the flow of grace, strength, and inspiration you released to me as I wrote this book. I couldn't have done it without your help. I love you H.S!

To my lovely husband, Emmanuel Adewusi, thank you for always being a shoulder I can lean on. Thank you for your encouragement, support, prayers, impartation of grace as I wrote this book. I am deeply grateful and I love you Sweetheart.

To my team that supported every aspect of the publishing of this book, I am immensely grateful. Your patience, expertise and willingness to ensure this book reaches the nations is greatly appreciated!

To every single ready to venture on an exciting journey of discovery and maximizing your single season.

Introduction

Every season has its unique characteristics embedded within it. We have the **Winter** season, where snow falls, temperatures drop, and hibernation peaks. Then comes the **Spring** season, where snow melts, light begins to break through long nights, and new plant growth emerges as temperatures rise. After a few months, **Summer** arrives. In summer, things get even brighter and more colourful as plants grow, people emerge from hibernation, and outdoor activities peak due to the warm temperatures. Sometimes people complain about the heat, but the **Fall/Autumn** season begins just in time. In the fall, leaves change to shades of yellow, orange, brown, and red, creating a beautiful collage.

While I prefer spring for its balance of hot and cold temperatures, every season has its own beauty. For example, winter kicks off a new year filled with excitement, renewed passion, and vision for the months ahead. Winter also offers adventurous activities like snowmobiling, snowboarding, and skiing. Spring brings rain, which may seem annoying but is essential for farmers and crops, contributing to our food supply. It is also a time to celebrate Easter, marking the immense sacrifice and love of Jesus Christ. Summer is known for its bright sunshine, drawing people to outdoor activities like festivals, hiking, horseback riding, and picnics. It is also peak season for weddings and graduations. As fall begins, we round up the year. It's a season of new school years, slight temperature drops, and beautiful fall fashion. Fall also fosters bonding and gatherings with loved ones as we celebrate Thanksgiving and Christmas.

Each season, though different, carries unique beauty and, when embraced, reveals its wonders. Similarly, every human will experience a single season. Many rush out of their single season, obsessed with the brightness of the married season, failing to realize that the single season also holds its own beauty. Ecclesiastes 3 reminds us that there is a time for everything and every season has its purpose:

"There is a season (a time appointed) for everything and a time for every delight and event or purpose under heaven... He has made everything beautiful and appropriate in its time. He has also planted eternity [a sense of divine purpose] in the human heart [a mysterious longing which nothing under the sun can satisfy, except God]—yet man cannot find out (comprehend, grasp) what God has done (His overall plan) from the beginning to the end." — (Ecclesiastes 3:1, 11, AMP)

My spiritual dad once said, "Just like we have to honour people and principles, we also have to honour seasons as well." If you honour a season, it will yield its sweet fruit and goodness. Likewise, being single is a season appointed by God, and when embraced and honoured, it yields beautiful fruits. Make the decision today to honour your single season. It is a season to be enjoyed, not endured! It is time to be singled out!

Section I

The Essence of Being Singled Out

Chapter 1

The Essence of Being Singled Out

What It Means to be Singled Out

According to the Cambridge Dictionary, to single someone/something out means *"to choose one person or thing from a group for special attention..."* My definition of being singled out is *"to be* **set apart, to stand out, to be chosen out of many by God."**

Some singles sometimes feel "left out" in their single season. **You are not left out but singled out!** There is a huge difference between these two concepts. Being *'left out'* signifies being abandoned or rejected. On the contrary, being *'singled out'* is when someone takes an interest in you and puts a special spotlight on you among the crowd. God is putting a divine spotlight on you as He singles you out of the crowd to prepare you for a desired future. This can be likened to a job posting many people have applied for. Out of the many applicants and interviews conducted, only one individual was singled out as a successful candidate for the position. Esther was singled out among so many young virgin ladies who were applying to be the next queen to King Xerxes, and amongst so many, the king's eunuch, Hegai, took a special interest in Esther without any ulterior motive and showered her with favour. To put things in context, Hegai was the eunuch in charge of the king's women and was probably knowledgeable about the king's preferences. When it was time for Esther to approach the king and take whatever she decided to the king's palace, Hegai advised her on exactly what to take, and when all saw her (including the king), she found favour in their sight, and it is no surprise that she was crowned the next queen.

8 So it came about when the king's command and his decree were proclaimed and when many young women were gathered together in the citadel of Susa into the custody of Hegai, that Esther was taken to the king's palace [and placed] in the custody of Hegai, who was in charge of the women. 9 Now the young woman pleased Hegai and found favor with him. So he quickly provided her with beauty preparations and her [portion of] food, and he gave her seven choice maids from the king's palace; then he transferred her and her maids to the best place in the harem." 12 Now when it was each young woman's turn to go before King Ahasuerus, after the end of her twelve months under the regulations for the women—for the days of their beautification were completed as follows: six months with oil of myrrh and six months with [sweet] spices and perfumes and the beauty preparations for women— 13 then the young woman would go before the king in this way: anything that she wanted was given her to take with her from the harem into the king's palace. 14 In the evening she would go in and the next morning she would return to the second harem, to the custody of Shaashgaz, the king's eunuch who was in charge of the concubines. She would not return to the king unless he delighted in her and she was summoned by name. 15 Now as for Esther, the daughter of Abihail the uncle of Mordecai who had taken her in as his [own] daughter, when her turn came to go in to the king, she requested nothing except what Hegai the king's eunuch [and attendant] who was in charge of the women, advised. And Esther found favor in the sight of all who saw her. 16 So Esther was taken to King Ahasuerus, to his royal palace in the tenth month, that is, the month of Tebeth (Dec-Jan), in the seventh year of his reign. **17 Now the king loved Esther more than all the other women, and she found favor and kindness with him more than all the [other] virgins, so that he set the royal crown on her head and made her queen in the place of Vashti.** *(Esther 2: 8-9, 12-17, AMP)*

What Being Single is NOT

A single person is someone who is yet to be married, which includes someone not in a romantic relationship, someone in a romantic relationship but not yet married, someone engaged but not yet married, someone who is divorced, or someone who is a widow and interested in remarrying. Let's dive into what being single is not.

It is not an Abomination to God

Some single people believe or perhaps have been treated as if they sinned against God, and this is God's way of punishing them. I'm here to tell you that is a lie from the pit of hell. There is nothing wrong with being in your single season, and it is not because God is angry with you and desires to punish you. Jeremiah 29:11 reminds us that God desires the very best for us, including those who are single.

"For I know the thoughts that I think toward you, says the Lord, thoughts of peace and not of evil, to give you a future and a hope." (Jeremiah 29:11, NKJV)

It is not a Disadvantage

Being single is not a disease or a disadvantage. In Ruth 1, Ruth experienced the loss of her husband and found herself being single again. Not only did she lose her husband but also her brother-in-law and her father-in-law. In those days, if a woman lost her husband, she had the chance of being married to her brother-in-law, but in her case, that was not an option. It might have seemed like she was at a disadvantage, but God had not given up on her. She carried on with her life and her purpose, which led her to glean in the field of Boaz. In those days, gleaning from other people's fields was a common practice, and as she gleaned, Boaz took notice of her upon his return. You can imagine that she was not the only one gleaning from the fields, yet she was singled out to be favoured by him.

1 In the days when the judges ruled in Israel, a severe famine came upon the land. So a man from Bethlehem in Judah left his home and went to live in the country of Moab, taking his wife and two sons with him. 2 The man's name was Elimelech, and his wife was Naomi. Their two sons were Mahlon and Kilion. They were Ephrathites from Bethlehem in the land of Judah. And when they reached Moab, they settled there. 3 Then Elimelech died, and Naomi was left with her two sons. 4 The two sons married Moabite women. One married a woman named Orpah, and the other a woman named Ruth. But about ten years later, 5 both Mahlon and Kilion died. This left Naomi alone, without her two sons or her husband. (Ruth 1:1-5, NLT)

One day Ruth the Moabite said to Naomi, "Let me go out into the harvest fields to pick up the stalks of grain left behind by anyone who is kind enough to let me do it. Naomi replied, "All right, my daughter, go ahead." 3 So Ruth went out to gather grain behind the harvesters. And as it happened, she found herself working in a field that belonged to Boaz, the relative of her father-in-law, Elimelech. 4 While she was there, Boaz arrived from Bethlehem and greeted the harvesters. "The Lord be with you!" he said. "The Lord bless you!" the harvesters replied. 5 Then Boaz asked his foreman, "Who is that young woman over there? Who does she belong to?" 6 And the foreman replied, "She is the young woman from Moab who came back with Naomi. 7 She asked me this morning if she could gather grain behind the harvesters. She has been hard at work ever since, except for a few minutes' rest in the shelter." 8 Boaz went over and said to Ruth, "Listen, my daughter. Stay right here with us when you gather grain; don't go to any other fields. Stay right behind the young women working in my field. 9 See which part of the field they are harvesting, and then follow them. I have warned the young men not to treat you roughly. And when you are thirsty, help yourself to the water they have drawn from the well." 10 Ruth fell at his feet and thanked him warmly. "What have I done to deserve such kindness?" she asked. "I am only a foreigner." (Ruth 2:2-10, NLT)

It is not a Waste of Time

Sometimes, you may encounter people who may put pressure on you, asking when you will get married, making it seem like you are losing time and not getting any younger. Seeing your colleagues getting married can also put pressure on you, but you must remember that there is time for everything, and every season is pregnant with its fruits and beauty. There are many things God wants to achieve and birth during your single season. Your single season is not a waste of time.

The Purpose of the Single Season

When a child is born, he/she undergoes a season where they depend on their parents for everything: food, clothing, shelter, etc. As they mature, they get into the independent stage, where they begin to fully discover who they are, their preferences, their dislikes, their personality, their passions, their vision, their values, and their belief systems. This purposeful season of discovery, understanding, building, and establishment is called the Single Season. God intentionally orchestrated this season to ensure the proper foundation is laid for the desired future God has in store for you.

In the following chapters, we will look at how to maximize the single season through the following steps:

1. **Building an Intimate Relationship with God**

2. **Dealing with Any trauma**

3. **Discovering and Understanding Your Design**

4. **Discovering and Running with Your Vision**

5. **Building Your Character**

6. **Visualizing Your Desired Future**

Let's dive in!

Section II

How to Maximize the Single Season

Chapter 2

Build an Intimate Relationship with God

We all have different kinds of relationships. One of such kind is what I call the "**Hi/Bye Relationship.**" These are relationships that are very surface and superficial. They are ones you don't go deep into with your conversations and perhaps only discuss "the weather," but nothing intimate. Another kind of relationship is the "**Intimate Relationship.**" With intimate relationships, there is depth in your interactions, and access is given to your heart. Likewise, it is possible to mirror the same in our relationships with God.

The Hi/Bye relationship with God might include attending church and serving, but that's where it stops. Yes, these individuals are present in His house, but their hearts are far from His heart. God is not given any access or governance into their lives. They might have even said the sinner's prayer and given their lives to Christ initially, but as life continued, they took their life back from Jesus Christ, removing His authority. Their relationship with Him is simply superficial and has no roots.

"You hypocrites! Isaiah was right when he prophesied about you, for he wrote, 'These people honor me with their lips, but their hearts are far from me.'" (Matthew 15:7-8, NLT)

God desires that we build an intimate relationship with Him. "To build" requires intentionality and focused investment. When a person desires to build a house, several costs, materials, time, and other resources must be considered to ensure the proper foundation is laid and that the structure built on the foundation is solid and secure. Many desire a wonderful romantic relationship with someone else, but the foundation of any human relationship starts with building an intimate relationship with God first!

"But seek first the kingdom of God and His righteousness, and all these things shall be added to you." (Matthew 6:33, NKJV)

From the above scripture, one of the 'added things' a person enjoys when they seek God first is a thriving relationship. I really love the book "The 5 Love Languages" by Gary Chapman because it helps us understand the different love languages of one's self and that of others. It also teaches how to effectively communicate our love to a person through their love languages. Some of the love languages mentioned in the book include **Words of Affirmation, Acts of Service, Quality Time, Gifts, and Physical Touch.**

It's no coincidence that we are made in the image and likeness of God. Just as humans have love languages, I truly believe God also has love languages. Understanding what they are will help us strengthen our connection with God and go deeper in intimacy with Him. We all desire to be loved, but God also longs for us to truly love Him from the bottom of our hearts. Let's examine how we can build intimacy and our love relationship with God.

God's Love Languages

Quality and Quantity Time

Time! Time! Time! This is one commodity we tend to say we don't have enough of, but the truth of the matter is that we create time for the things we value the most. My spiritual dad has said that 'there are competing visions in life'; but what we decide to create time for truly shows how valuable it is to us. When you love someone, you will want to spend time with them. God desires to spend time with us. He doesn't just want to spend time with us, but He desires to spend **quality** time where the attention we give Him is undivided.

You may feel disrespected when you are trying to have a serious conversation with someone who is distracted and more interested in what's happening on their phone. They keep checking their phone to see if there are any new text messages or scrolling through their Instagram feed while the conversation is ongoing. If you have experienced this before, it leaves a really bitter taste in your mouth. Do you know that's the same way God sometimes feels about us?

When God created Adam and Eve in the Garden of Eden, one of the first ways He directly showed His love was by spending quality time with them.

"When the cool evening breezes were blowing, the man and his wife heard the Lord God walking about in the garden. So they hid from the Lord God among the trees. Then the Lord God called to the man, 'Where are you?'" (Genesis 3:8-9, NLT)

There was a set time and place when God and man (Adam and Eve) communed together, and they were nowhere to be found when God arrived at the right time. Notice how God did not choose to come when the heat of the day was up. Instead, He chose to arrive when the cool evening breezes were blowing. This must have been intentional, as the heat of the day itself could be a distraction. Instead, God may have wanted a peaceful atmosphere, ensuring that nothing interrupted His time with Adam and Eve.

Now, I'm not saying you only have to commune with God in the evening but find a time and place where you are not distracted by your devices, people, tasks, or anything physical or mental. To many people, God is asking, **"Where are you?"** Quality time with God isn't a thing of the past; He still longs to spend quality time with us today. In James 4:8, He reminds us of His yearning, *"Draw near to God and He will draw near to you..."* (NKJV)

We can demonstrate to God in many ways that we desire to spend quality time with Him. For example, if worship is your channel of grace (your channel to connect with God), play some anointed music in the background and start worshiping God. As you do this, you will notice a shift as you begin to connect with Him. This may result in you bursting out in prayer, reading His word, meditating on His words (written or spoken), or the Holy Spirit may begin to speak to you. God intentionally put His Spirit (the Holy Spirit) in us to ensure we are in constant communion with Him.

It is not enough to just have quality time with God in one instance and then wait months or a year before God hears from us again. He also desires **quantity** time with us, where the connection and interaction He has with us never ends.

*"He who **dwells** in the **secret** place of the Most High shall abide under the shadow of the Almighty."* (Psalms 91:1, NKJV)

To "dwell" in the above scripture means to stay. It means you are not in a rush. There is a difference between an Airbnb space and your House. An Airbnb is a temporary lodging space with a limited stay before you must check out. On the other hand, your house is more permanent and allows you to dwell and stay longer. Likewise, God desires for us to dwell in His presence and not have a drive-thru experience with Him. Secrets are revealed to those who dwell.

It is impossible to have constant communion with God if you have not surrendered your heart to Jesus Christ. He is so excited to start a conversation with you with no divided attention. If you would like to join Him in this journey of sweet communion today, please turn to the end of the book to repeat the sinner's prayer with me.

Words of Affirmation

Someone whose love language is Words of Affirmation appreciates compliments and kind words. Can you remember the last time you received a captivating text from someone you love—perhaps a spouse, a romantic partner, or a friend—expressing their love for you and the reasons behind it? Remember how you smiled uncontrollably, leaving others puzzled by your sudden happiness? Days afterward, that text replayed in your mind, and each time you thought about it, you couldn't help but smile. That's the same feeling God has when we praise, worship, and give Him thanks.

Psalms 100:4 says, *"Enter into His gates with thanksgiving, And into His courts with praise. Be thankful to Him, and bless His name."* (NKJV) In some places in Africa, during a ceremony, there are bands that play different instruments. One particular instrument, called the "Talking Drum," seems to "talk" through the instrumentalists' words as they sing praises. As they play, your spirit is lifted, and you feel so filled with joy that you're excited to tip them generously. Why? Because of the words of affirmation sung about you.

It's the same when we praise God from the depths of our hearts. When we thank Him for what He has done, is doing, and will do in our lives and worship Him for who He is, this truly exalts God. No wonder David says in Psalms 22:3, *"Yet I know that you are most holy; it's indisputable. You are God-Enthroned, surrounded with songs, living among the shouts of praise of your princely people."* (TPT) David understood how to express words of affirmation to God. Much of the Book of Psalms consists of words of affirmation to God, and we see God refer to David as a man after His own heart. Words of Affirmation to God touch the very heart of God. You may be wondering if David was manipulating God by using words of affirmation, but it would be an insult to think we can trick God without Him being aware. God is seeking those who worship Him in spirit and in **truth** (John 4:23).

Reasons to Praise God

I used to wonder why God needed us to praise Him, given that He has angels and the heavenly 24 elders singing His praise continuously (Revelation 19). Here are a few reasons why we need to praise Him:

We Are Made in His Image and Likeness

We are the only creation made in the image and likeness of God. This is a significant honour because we carry the very DNA of God Almighty, the Master of the universe. There is none who can compare to Him, and yet we are made in His image and likeness.

We Were Created to Praise Him

In 1 Peter 2:9, it says, *"But you are a chosen generation, a royal priesthood, a holy nation, His own special people, that you may proclaim the praises of Him who called you out of darkness into His marvelous light [.]"* (NKJV) The purpose behind our creation is to exalt and magnify God.

We Are Redeemed from Darkness to Light

We have been redeemed from the kingdom of darkness into the kingdom of light. Our praise is a response to this incredible act of salvation.

If We Don't Praise Him, Stones Will

Luke 19:40 mentions how if no one praises Him, the stones will break forth with praise. There is a praise tank allotted for us to fill with our praises to God. This praise should come from a willing heart. We are more significant than stones, but if the "special people of God" are not willing to praise Him, then something as insignificant as stones will take our place. God forbid!

Let's make the decision today to fill God's love tank with words of affirmation from the bottom of our hearts.

Gifts

Remember Abraham in the Bible, who waited 25 years for his promised son, and finally, Isaac arrived! Only for God to ask this of him: *"Take your son, your only son—yes, Isaac, whom you love so much—and go to the land of Moriah. Go and sacrifice him as a burnt offering on one of the mountains which I will show you."* (Genesis 22:2, NLT) Notice how God specifically refers to Isaac and not Ishmael to prevent any misunderstanding. God also emphasizes how much Abraham loves Isaac, which is understandable after waiting 25 long years!

Look at verse 3: *"The next morning Abraham got up early. He saddled his donkey and took two of his servants with him, along with his son, Isaac. Then he chopped wood for a fire for a burnt offering and set out for the place God had told him about."* (Genesis 22:3, NLT) There was no hesitation, delay, or complaining—just pure obedience. As Abraham was about to kill his son as a sacrifice according to instructions, the angel of the Lord called out to him, instructing him not to lay a hand on the boy or hurt him in any way.

Look at what God says to Abraham: *"Because you have obeyed me and have not withheld even your son, your only son, I swear by my own name that I will certainly bless you. I will multiply your descendants beyond number, like the stars in the sky and the sand on the seashore. Your descendants will conquer the cities of their enemies. And through your descendants, all the nations of the earth will be blessed—all because you have obeyed me."*(Genesis 22:16-18, NLT) This act of giving deeply moved God. Not only because Abraham, a mere human like you and I, obeyed God, but this was a glimpse into what God had decided to do for us by giving His only begotten Son to the world (John 3:16). The highest level of giving is sacrifice!

God has given us the greatest gift any human could ever ask for, all because He loves us. On the flip side, what are we willing to give to God? Someone once said, "It is possible to give without loving, but impossible to love without giving." We show our love for God when we cheerfully give to Him (2 Corinthians 9:7). This could be our material resources like money, time, talents, or skills, among many others. Nothing should be off-limits for us to give to God Almighty if we truly love Him! The greatest gift anyone can give to God is sacrificing their life to Jesus Christ by allowing Him to govern every affair of their lives without any limit.

Acts of Service

In many countries, November 11 is Remembrance Day, a day set aside to commemorate and honour the sacrifices made by those who have dedicated and are still dedicating their lives to service for their country. It has cost many their lives, time, and comfort, among many other things. If you ask any veteran why they decided to serve, many will say it is because of their love for their country.

Love is such a powerful virtue, and the story of Jacob and Rachel gives us a glimpse into this attribute. In Genesis 29, Jacob was lovestruck when he set his eyes on Rachel at the well. He was ready to work seven years for Rachel's father, Laban, in exchange for having her as his wife. Genesis 29:20 says, *"So Jacob worked seven years to pay for Rachel. But his love for her was so strong that it seemed to him but a few days."* (NLT) Wow, it had to be love in operation for a person to work without any pay but only in exchange for a lady he loved. Unfortunately, his father-in-law tricked him and gave her older sister, Leah, to Jacob instead of Rachel. Because of his love for Rachel, he was willing to work __another__ seven years for her, totalling **14 years!**

Our acts of service to God demonstrate our love for Him. This could be serving at your local church or any organization or activity focused on furthering the kingdom of God. God is not interested in us merely providing a service; He desires it to be wholehearted and genuine, motivated by love. Deuteronomy 10:12 says:

"And now, Israel, what does the Lord your God require of you? He requires only that you fear the Lord your God, and live in a way that pleases Him, and love Him and serve Him with all your heart and soul." (NLT)

You may have visited a restaurant where you encountered a server who did a great job waiting on your table, going the extra mile for you, and doing so with a genuine smile (not the quick on-and-off smile). You might have been so pleased and eager to give them a big tip at the end of your visit. On the other hand, you may have encountered a different server who seemed angry because you visited the restaurant and gave you an attitude whenever you asked to clarify a menu option. At the end of your visit, it would only take God's grace to tip such a server because of their attitude. Yes, they served you, but the attitude was not pleasant. What attitude do we have when we serve God? Do we grumble and complain when serving God? Do we do careless and casual jobs in whatever area we serve? Or do we serve God with excellence, diligence, consistency, and joy? Let's decide to serve God with everything we have: our resources, our time, our talents, our passion, and, more importantly, our life! Let our service be a sweet aroma before God, one He will delight in.

You have a choice, but just like Joshua, let's decide that we and our families will serve the Lord!

"And if it seems evil to you to serve the Lord, choose for yourselves this day whom you will serve, whether the gods which your fathers served that were on the other side of the River, or the gods of the Amorites, in whose land you dwell. But as for me and my house, we will serve the Lord." (Joshua 24:15, NKJV)

Touch

The heartbeat of God's heart is souls. Souls are very dear to Him because He desires to see everyone reconnect with Him. Just like the father of the prodigal son in the parable found in Luke 15:11-32, God longs for His lost children to come back home and rekindle their relationship with Him. One way we touch the heart of God is by winning souls back to His kingdom. This brings immense joy to His heart. Just as the prodigal son's father launched a party for his son's return, the same happens in heaven when a soul is translated from the kingdom of darkness into God's marvellous light.

"I say to you that likewise there will be more joy in heaven over one sinner who repents than over ninety-nine just persons who need no repentance." (Luke 15:7, NKJV)

God needs us as His hands and feet to accomplish this mission of reconciliation. Just as someone attaches a finder's fee to an item they have lost, signifying its preciousness, God attaches a reward to those who win souls for His kingdom.

*"The fruit of the righteous is a tree of life, And he who wins souls is **wise**."* (Proverbs 11:30, NKJV)

*"Those who are **wise** shall shine like the brightness of the firmament, and those who turn many to righteousness, like the stars forever and ever."* (Daniel 12:3, NKJV)

When we win souls for Him, we express our love for what matters most to God—souls—and hence, we touch His very heart.

Chapter 3

Deal With Any Trauma

Understanding Trauma: The Excess Baggage

Have you ever been at the airline counter, ready to check in your bags, only for the airline agent to inform you that your bags exceed the allowed weight? In such a case, you have two choices: get rid of the excess baggage or pay for the extra weight. Trauma can be likened to this excess baggage. You must either let go of it or pay the costly price of holding onto it.

According to the American Psychological Association, trauma is an emotional response to a terrible event such as an accident, assault, or natural disaster. Immediate responses can include shock or denial. Long-term reactions might encompass unpredictable emotions, flashbacks, strained relationships, and even physical symptoms like headaches or nausea (2008).

3 Categories of Trauma

As outlined by the Missouri Department of Elementary and Secondary Education, there are three categories of trauma:

Acute Trauma

This type of trauma is based on a single incident—for example, the death of a loved one.

Chronic Trauma

This trauma results from repeated or prolonged terrible incidents, such as recurring domestic violence or abuse.

Complex Trauma

This type of trauma occurs when a person is exposed to various or multiple traumatic events, creating a cocktail of several terrible incidents.

Forms of Trauma

Primary Trauma

This is when a traumatic event happens directly to an individual.

Secondary Trauma

This is when a traumatic event happens indirectly to an individual. For example, witnessing someone else undergo a traumatic event, such as a child witnessing one of their parents go through domestic violence.

Different Trauma Responses

When faced with a threatening situation, individuals may respond differently as coping mechanisms. Let's explore some responses to trauma:

Fight Response

This is a defensive reaction to a threatening incident for self-preservation or protection. In this response, an individual aggressively confronts the perceived danger or threat, intending to overpower or neutralize it.

Some fight responses might include:

- Impulsivity and hypersensitivity, such as immediately pushing someone away who touches you

- Physically defending oneself from a threat

- Glaring at someone or using a biting tone

- Shouting "No!" when someone doesn't leave you alone

- Telling someone you weren't responsible for something they blamed you for

- Trying to prove you are right or perpetuating an argument after it's over

- Assigning yourself the role of leader, dictating the space you're in

- Self-sabotage: starting fights with someone over insignificant or invented situations (Mountainside Treatment Center)

Flight Response

This trauma response is to avoid or run away from the perceived danger or threat. Individuals might isolate themselves through avoidant behaviours to distance themselves from threatening situations.

Some flight responses include:

- Running away from perceived danger, such as loud bangs in public

- Leaning on perfectionism to avoid criticism

- Becoming a workaholic to distract oneself

- Positioning oneself to face the exit in a restaurant or other crowded room

- Difficulty focusing on anything but thoughts of the trigger

- Difficulty resting, relaxing the body, and falling asleep

- Hypervigilance and jumpiness

- Racing or obsessive thoughts

- Using substances such as drugs and alcohol to dampen anxiety (Mountainside Treatment Center)

Freeze Response

This is a trauma response characterized by passivity or numbness toward a perceived threat or danger. Individuals detach from reality and may experience a blackout or loss of functioning emotionally, physiologically, or physically, such as immobility in the presence of danger. For example, someone might see a moving vehicle coming towards them and suddenly go into shock and freeze.

Some freeze responses may include:

- Difficulty expressing emotions, such as using a monotone voice
- Selective mutism or going non-verbal under stress
- Making choices becomes harder, leading to decision fatigue
- Brain fog: confusion, forgetfulness, attention issues
- Leaving conversations without clarity
- Depression and hibernation
- Struggling to make plans or stick to them
- Periods of inactivity
- Constantly daydreaming
- Not answering the phone and avoiding conversations about your needs
- Escaping reality through addictions such as marijuana, alcohol, video games, or television (Mountainside Treatment Center)

Fawn Response

This is a trauma response where individuals try to avoid conflict with the threat or danger by seeking favour through flattery or exaggerated attentiveness. They aim to please whoever they perceive as a threat, especially after a failed attempt at a fight, flight or freeze response. Consequently, they prioritize the threat and its needs over their own, mirroring a co-dependent relationship. For example, someone in a toxic or abusive relationship might try to soothe their attacker's temper by doing whatever the attacker wants. This is sometimes seen with rape victims, particularly those who have been kidnapped, as they begin to see their kidnapper or rapist as a lover, as a means to cope with the situation and prevent further harm.

Some examples of fawn responses include:

- Having a hard time saying "no"

- Over-apologizing or accepting blame for something you did not do

- Assuming you are responsible for others' emotions

- Prioritizing someone over yourself, even abandoning your plans to be with them

- Lacking a sense of self or having a hard time describing yourself

- Changing your preferences, such as personal style and hobbies, to match someone else's

- Flattering others

- Defending people who hurt you and staying in toxic or abusive situations

- Choosing a career path to please family members

- Following commands without considering your own wants (Mountainside Treatment Center)

Common Causes of Trauma

Below are some common causes of trauma, but this list is not exhaustive:

- Death

- Domestic Violence or Physical Abuse

- Verbal Abuse

- Sexual Abuse

- Infidelity

- Rejection or Abandonment

- Authority Figures (e.g., teachers, parents, church leaders, bosses, etc.)

Examples of People Who Experienced Trauma

David

David experienced multiple traumas throughout his life, including:

Trauma with his Father and Siblings

During the visit of the prophet Samuel, who came to select a king from the sons of Jesse, David was not informed of the prophet's visit until God intervened (1 Samuel 16). This act of negligence could traumatize a child, sending the signal that he was not significant enough to be included in such an important event.

Trauma with an Authority Figure

King Saul was someone David looked up to as a father figure and even referred to as "father." However, due to King Saul's insecurity, he saw David as an enemy and aimed to kill him for the rest of David's life. *"Look, my father, at what I have in my hand. It is a piece of the hem of your robe! I cut it off, but I didn't kill you. This proves that I am not trying to harm you and that I have not sinned against you, even though you have been hunting for me to kill me."* (1 Samuel 24:11, NLT) David experienced physical and emotional abuse at the hands of King Saul.

Trauma with his Son

Many times, people are more aware of the trauma caused by parents to children, but children can also traumatize their parents. In the case of David, his son Absalom did outrageous things, including sleeping with his wives and attempting to overthrow him. This caused deep pain in David's heart, seeing his son turn against him.

Naomi

The death of her husband and later her two sons within a short span was highly traumatic for Naomi. The loss of her loved ones was so overwhelming that, even though her name meant "sweet," she renamed herself "bitter."

"She said to them, 'Do not call me Naomi (sweetness); call me Mara (bitter), for the Almighty has caused me great grief and bitterness.'" (Ruth 1:20, AMP)

Rachel

The pain and stress of childbirth were so intense that Rachel was willing to change the destiny of her son by naming him "Benoni" (son of sorrow), until Jacob canceled it and renamed him "Benjamin" (son of my right hand). Remember, it took a long time for Rachel to give birth, and now, as she was giving birth to her second son, she was traumatized by the experience. If you have experienced such trauma before, during, or after delivery, it is important to address it.

Tamar

This sibling trauma involved sexual abuse committed against Tamar by her half-brother, despite her pleas for him not to commit such an atrocity (2 Samuel 13).

Absalom

Absalom was a secondary victim of the rape of his sister, Tamar. Although he did not experience the trauma primarily, witnessing his sister's trauma affected him deeply. Because his trauma was never addressed, it eventually led him to kill his brother Amnon and engage in other atrocities against his father, who never addressed the rape committed against Tamar (2 Samuel 13).

Joseph

He was sold into slavery by his brothers. Not only was this traumatizing, but he was also falsely accused by Potiphar's wife, which landed him in prison for several years. This was a mixture of trauma induced by family and authoritative figures.

"Speaking among themselves, they said, 'Clearly we are being punished because of what we did to Joseph long ago.

We saw his anguish when he pleaded for his life, but we wouldn't listen. That's why we're in this trouble.'" (Genesis 42:21, NLT)

Moses

Due to orders issued at his birth, Moses was abandoned and raised by someone else (Pharaoh's daughter). Although his mother was involved in his life as he grew up, this left a sense of abandonment in Moses. Additionally, he was further rejected by the Israelites he fought for, who accused him of being a murderer, causing him to flee from Egypt for several years (Exodus 2).

You may relate to any of the above examples or perhaps none, but it is crucial to identify any form of trauma you might have experienced and determine how to address it.

Characteristics of Trauma and The Importance of Addressing It

Trauma Affects a Person's Sense of Security and Safety

When a person has undergone a traumatic experience, it affects their sense of safety and security, making them feel vulnerable physically, emotionally, mentally, and even spiritually.

Physical Insecurity

For example, someone who has been raped or gone through domestic violence has had their physical body mishandled and abused. As a result, they may feel unsafe around men if it was a woman who experienced rape or domestic violence, and vice versa.

Emotional Insecurity

An individual who has experienced a traumatic event may feel exposed emotionally and thus tend to close off emotionally. This affects their response to displays of love as a way to prevent further emotional pain. For example, a child who was rejected or abandoned might find it challenging to accept or receive love, and consequently, they may also be closed off from giving love themselves.

Mental Insecurity

Trauma distorts reality and skews the way individuals begin to view themselves. For example, a person who has undergone gaslighting may start to believe the lies and falsehoods presented by the abuser. This act messes with their thinking and self-perception, leading them to lose confidence in how they view or think of themselves.

Spiritual Insecurity

When a terrible incident occurs, people often wonder where God was during such an atrocity, creating a false view of God and His love toward them. This can also happen when a traumatic incident involves, directly or indirectly, a spiritual leader who represents God. This is where perceived or actual church trauma comes into play, leading individuals to feel unsafe around anything involving God or a spiritual leader.

Trauma Affects a Person's Perspective of Love

One way to recognize if someone is traumatized is how they respond to love. Their response to displays of love from God, others, or even themselves can manifest as either rejection or obsession. Trauma pushes a person to extremes: they might reject every display of love or become obsessed with being loved, even if the love is unhealthy or toxic. For example, King David was traumatized by rejection from spiritual authorities, causing him to cling to anyone who offered him love. When his daughter

Tamar was raped, addressing it might have led to losing the love of his son Amnon. Instead, David didn't address it, which contributed to creating a destructive path for Absalom.

Trauma Can Impact Witnesses of a Traumatic Event

Trauma does not only affect the primary victim but can also have a significant impact on secondary victims—those who witness a traumatic event or see someone else being traumatized. Just like second-hand smoke affects a person's lungs, secondary trauma also has a detrimental impact. For instance, Absalom was a secondary victim of the sexual abuse of his sister Tamar.

Trauma Fixates a Person on an Event or the Past

When someone undergoes a traumatic incident, shock is an immediate response. Even if they physically recover from the shock, they often remain emotionally and mentally fixated on the past. This can lead to stagnation, causing an adult to still feel like a child emotionally and mentally due to unresolved childhood trauma. For example, many adult sex offenders were molested when young and never dealt with it, keeping them mentally in their childhood.

Trauma Varies Per Person

What might be traumatic for one person may not necessarily be for another. Therefore, it is essential not to belittle or dismiss an individual's traumatic experiences.

Trauma Can Be Reproduced or Transferred to Future Generations

Unaddressed trauma has the potential to reproduce itself in others, perpetuating a cycle where the traumatized person ends up traumatizing others. The saying "hurt people, hurt others" reflects this reality. For instance, Absalom, hurting from Tamar's rape, took matters into his own hands, traumatized Amnon by killing him, and traumatically impacted his father, King David, by sleeping with his wives and attempting to overthrow him. Anger is a common sign of intergenerational trauma.

Trauma Can Alter a Person's Personality and Identity

An individual whose original personality is outgoing and jovial might withdraw and become quiet, which could be a sign of trauma.

Word to Parents and Caregivers: Something might be wrong if you notice a child (or someone you know) who is usually lively becoming quiet or isolating themselves. Please do not ignore this. Speak with them and explore whether any traumatic event has taken place.

How to Deal with Trauma

Speak with Someone Equipped to Handle Trauma

Finding someone who is qualified to help you process and heal from trauma is crucial. This could be a counsellor, therapist, or pastor who you consider a safe place and someone you trust. Ensure that the person is adequately equipped to deal with trauma to ensure your session is effective and you adequately address any traumatic experiences.

Additional Resources

An excellent resource for addressing trauma is *"Overcoming Trauma,"* preached by Apostle Emmanuel Adewusi at Cornerstone Christian Church of God, available on YouTube. Take a listen!

Chapter 4

Discover and Understand Your Design

I recall watching a documentary about the Rolls Royce car brand and how meticulously they manufactured one of their models, the Celestial Phantom. This bespoke model features 446 diamonds; each precisely hand-set into specific car parts. There was so much precision, gentleness, and care involved in placing the diamonds by hand (not machine-assisted) that each diamond was examined to ensure it was correctly set. If not, they would start again from the top. This white-glove service reminds me of Psalm 139, which gives us an idea of the meticulous care and attention God put into our creation. He did not mass-produce us but ensured that every aspect of our design was thoroughly thought out and crafted to create a masterpiece. We are limited editions because there is only one copy of us. No two human beings share the same fingerprints because we are a limited edition.

Self-Dating

To discover and understand your uniqueness, it is crucial to self-date. Self-dating means getting to know yourself better, including your likes or preferences, pet peeves, strengths, abilities, areas for improvement, weaknesses, personality type, and biblical character. Many want to skip the single season and jump into a relationship, expecting their partner to understand them. Unfortunately, they lack an understanding of who they truly are. Your design is very unique and different from that of other human beings, so it is important to self-date during the single season before dating other people. This gives you the ability and time to discover and understand the uniqueness God has placed inside you. However, if you're already in a relationship, it's never too late to begin the process of self-dating.

Let's dive into areas of our design that we need to discover and understand through self-dating.

Discover and Understand Your Personality Type

The way we view, interpret and interact with the world and people around us is influenced by our personality. George J. Boelcke wrote a fantastic book titled *Colorful Personalities: Discover Your Personality Type Through the Power of Colors*. This book breaks down personalities into four types using colours: Blues, Golds, Oranges, and Greens. Let's explore some characteristics of each personality type described by Boelcke.

Blues

Blues are individuals focused on building relationships. They naturally connect with others, making people feel seen, heard, welcomed, and special. Blues can spot someone sitting alone and start a friendly conversation with them. If you've met someone for the first time and felt like you've known them for ages because of the warmth and sincere care you felt while speaking with them, you likely met a Blue. They prefer in-person meetings to emails to pick up on non-verbal cues, and they appreciate being listened to with an open heart more than being offered solutions.

Strengths: Friendly, caring, great listeners, empathetic, joyful, forgiving, compassionate, team builders.

Golds

Golds are individuals who have a strong sense of duty and take their responsibilities very seriously. This is one reason why Golds are often the most loyal and long-term friends, employees, or volunteers. They have a strong sense of commitment to whatever has been entrusted to them, whether tasks or relationships, making them very supportive, trustworthy, and loyal. Truly, their word is their bond, and they will do whatever it takes to fulfill their commitment. Even if they accept an overload of responsibilities when they should have said no, they adhere to their commitments and view it as a lesson for the future. They are reliable individuals on whom you can depend without worry.

Planning and organizing are very important to Golds; hence, they tend to have a to-do list for most things. This helps them stick to their commitments and ensures nothing falls through the cracks. Checking off items on their to-do lists gives them a sense of accomplishment and victory. To plan and organize effectively, punctuality is crucial; for Golds, being on time is very important. They can be hard on themselves and others when time commitments are not met promptly. Being late to a meeting or an appointment tells them you do not respect or value their time. As such, excessive small talk, line-ups, lack of organization, or last-minute changes in plans frustrate or stress them out, as these are seen as time-wasters. Therefore, having things scheduled in their calendars or setting up a reminder system is essential for Golds.

Strengths: Accurate, detail-oriented, conscientious, loyal, punctual, strong-willed, thorough, focused, generous and helpful, organized and plan-oriented, stable and structured, and committed to family and friends.

Oranges

Oranges are typically the life of the party or room. They have a great sense of humour, an enthusiastic attitude, and a playful nature. They enjoy being noticed and recognized and are comfortable in the spotlight or center of attention. Oranges value freedom and resist too much routine or planning, contributing to their creativity and ability to think outside the box. This creative ability opens up a wide range of job opportunities for them in fields requiring innovation, such as renovation businesses, interior design, fashion design, and construction. They can think on their feet and easily adapt to last-minute changes, making them very flexible. They love competition, and their quick thinking makes them excellent salespeople or marketers.

Oranges thrive in social settings and are very friendly and approachable. When you speak with them for the first time, it often feels like you've known them for years. Their easy-going, fun, and humorous nature makes them enjoyable companions and great friends. They have a unique ability to make anyone and everyone feel comfortable around them, often making people feel like they are best friends. Oranges excel at networking and are often the go-to person for connections because of their extensive circle of friends and contacts.

Strengths: Energetic, spontaneous, open-minded, magnetic, risk-taker, social, flexible, adventurous, generous, attention-loving, and optimistic.

Greens

Individuals with the Green personality type have a thirst for knowledge and understanding. They possess a sharp mind and a strong desire to grow through their unending yearning to learn. Often visionaries, Greens are several steps ahead of others in their plans, ideas, and visions. They take joy in tackling the challenges they encounter and thrive as logical thinkers. They excel in creating and refining effective systems, whether in processes, the people they work with, or the structure of their environment.

Greens deeply care and have profound emotions, but they manifest these differently than other personality types. For example, when Greens are hurt, they prefer to be alone and sometimes turn to their computer, tablet, or other technological gadgets. They rarely express their feelings in public, including public displays of affection or verbal affirmations, unless they have learned these behaviours. Having "green time" is crucial for them, providing a great avenue to unwind alone, think through things, process information, strategize, or solve problems. Unfortunately, this need for alone time can sometimes be misunderstood by partners, family, or friends as being anti-social, but it is essential for them to recharge and relax.

Strengths: Analytical, logical, enjoy their own company, problem solvers, visionaries, not overly emotional, inquisitive, future-oriented, direct, well-read and have diverse interests

Embrace Self-Discovery

Discovering your personality type gives you a fresh appreciation for who you are and helps you understand your behaviour while identifying areas for improvement. George J. Boelcke's book offers a personality assessment test, which provides a great starting point for discovering and understanding your personality. This also lays a foundation for understanding other people's personalities, fostering better interactions and connections.

Discover and Understand Your Strengths and Abilities

I recall when I initially met my husband, he asked me about my skills, and I told him I didn't have any. I said, "I think God skipped me when giving people skills," and I honestly meant it. He was shocked at my response and reassured me that God never creates empty people. His words planted a seed that began the journey of discovering the unique strengths and abilities God had placed inside me.

My experience can be likened to the widow who approached Elisha with the concern that creditors were about to take her sons as slaves to repay her deceased husband's debt. When Elisha asked what she had in the house, she responded:

"So Elisha said to her, 'What shall I do for you? Tell me, what do you have in the house?' And she said, 'Your maidser-

vant has nothing in the house but a jar of oil.'" (2 Kings 4:2, NKJV)

In her eyes, the jar of oil seemed insignificant, almost nothing. Elisha then instructed her to borrow as many empty vessels as she could from her neighbours, shut the door behind her and her sons, and pour oil from the jar into the empty vessels, setting aside the full ones.

"Then he said, 'Go, borrow vessels from everywhere, from all your neighbors—empty vessels; do not gather just a few. And when you have come in, you shall shut the door behind you and your sons; then pour it into all those vessels, and set aside the full ones.'" (2 Kings 4:3-4, NKJV)

Desperate, the widow followed Elisha's instructions without question.

"So she went from him and shut the door behind her and her sons, who brought the vessels to her; and she poured it out. Now it came to pass, when the vessels were full, that she said to her son, 'Bring me another vessel.' And he said to her, 'There is not another vessel.' So the oil ceased. Then she came and told the man of God. And he said, 'Go, sell the oil and pay your debt; and you and your sons live on the rest.'" (2 Kings 4:5-7, NKJV)

Out of what seemed like a "less than nothing" jar of oil came multiple vessels filled with oil, enough to pay off her debts and provide for her family.

Like the widow and her jar of oil, I discovered one of my unique strengths—organization. I had assumed everyone had this gift until I realized otherwise. What seemed insignificant to me launched my career in event management and birthed my own business, ending years of unpaid work.

Your story might be similar to mine or just like the widow's, but I can guarantee you God never creates anyone empty! What you might think is insignificant could be destined to be your cornerstone. Tyler Perry, for example, knew he had a gift for writing, which led to stage plays, movies, sitcoms, and his own studios. Rowan Atkinson, famously known as Mr. Bean, started with a simple student sketch involving facial contortions and manic comedy, which led him to fame. You are NOT created empty! Every seed God has planted in you can lead you to your ordained destiny if you take the time to discover and understand your unique strengths and abilities.

Practical Ways to Discover Your Strengths and Abilities

Self-Assessment

Observe what comes naturally to you without effort. For instance, I discovered my knack for storytelling by noticing how animated and engaging my stories were, which helped me when presenting or ministering. Take note of what you do effortlessly and enjoy. Then, document these observations for frequent reference.

Reflect on Positive Feedback from Others

Pay attention to recurring positive comments and feedback you receive. This can help identify your unique qualities and areas where you excel. For example, if people frequently compliment your fashion sense, this could indicate a talent for creating stylish looks, potentially valuable in careers like fashion, interior design, or graphic design.

Seek Feedback from the Holy Spirit

The Holy Spirit, known as the Spirit of Truth (John 16:13), can reveal deep truths about your strengths that neither you nor others might be aware of, providing a holistic understanding of your abilities.

Experiment and Explore

Combine self-observation and positive feedback by experimenting with different activities and roles. If people compliment your fashion sense, try exploring fashion-related hobbies or projects to see how you can develop and utilize this talent.

Discovering your strengths and abilities will help you appreciate who you are and understand why you behave the way you do while also identifying areas for improvement. George J. Boelcke's book *Colorful Personalities* includes a personality assessment test, which can provide a great starting point for this journey. Embracing these natural talents can open up numerous opportunities and pathways in life.

Discover and Understand Your Preferences and Pet Peeves

Just as discovering our strengths and abilities is vital for personal growth, understanding our preferences and pet peeves is equally important. By identifying what you enjoy and what irritates you, this self-awareness helps you make informed decisions that align with your true self, leading to greater satisfaction, well-being, and fulfillment. Let's explore how to discover and understand these aspects of your design.

Practical Ways to Discover Your Preferences and Pet Peeves

Reflect on Your Daily Experiences

Take some time each day to reflect on your experiences. Pay attention to moments that brought you joy and those that caused frustration. Keeping a journal can be a helpful way to track these instances and identify patterns over time. For example, I noticed I have a strong preference for food presentation that is appealing to the eyes. Meals that are beautifully arranged not only enhance my dining experience but also excite me.

Seek Feedback from Others

Sometimes, those around us can provide valuable insights into our preferences and pet peeves. Ask friends, family, or colleagues to share their observations about what you seem to enjoy and what tends to annoy you. Their perspective can offer a fresh look at your behaviours and reactions. You might discover, for instance, that your friends often compliment your knack for choosing aesthetically pleasing restaurants, reflecting your preference for visually appealing environments.

Experiment with New Activities

Trying new activities can reveal preferences you might not have been aware of. Step out of your comfort zone and engage in different hobbies, volunteer opportunities, or social events. Notice which experiences you find fulfilling and which ones you don't enjoy as much. For instance, you might find that you enjoy organizing events because it allows you to create visually stunning setups that align with your preference for aesthetics.

Analyze Your Reactions

Pay close attention to your emotional responses in various situations. When you feel particularly happy or irritated, ask yourself why. Understanding the underlying reasons for these emotions can help you pinpoint specific preferences and pet peeves. For example, you might find that disorganized spaces frustrate you, while clean, orderly environments make you feel at peace.

Identify Common Themes

Look for common themes in your reflections and feedback. Do you feel energized by creative activities? Are you easily annoyed by disorganization? Identifying these themes can help you understand your core preferences and pet peeves. For example, you might notice a pattern where visual appeal plays a significant role in your enjoyment of activities, whether it's in food, fashion, or interior design.

Prioritize Your Preferences

Once you clearly understand your preferences, prioritize them in your daily life. Make time for activities and experiences that bring you joy. Surround yourself with environments and people that align with your values and interests. For example, if you love visually appealing food, you could make an effort to prepare and present your meals beautifully or dine at restaurants known for their artistic presentations.

Manage Your Pet Peeves

While it's important to focus on your preferences, acknowledging and managing your pet peeves is also crucial. Identify ways to minimize or cope with situations that irritate you. This might involve setting boundaries, developing coping strategies, or making small changes to your environment. If disorganization bothers you, creating a system to keep your space tidy can significantly reduce your stress.

Revisit and Revise

As you grow and change, your preferences and pet peeves might evolve. Periodically revisit your reflections and update your understanding. Stay flexible and open to discovering new aspects of yourself. Your appreciation for visually appealing food might expand to other areas like art or design, enriching your life further.

Exploring and understanding your preferences and pet peeves can give you valuable insights into your personality and design. Just as our strengths and abilities shape our paths, so too do our likes and dislikes guide us toward environments and experiences that resonate with our true selves. This leads to a more authentic and fulfilling life.

Discover and Understand Your Biblical Character/Persona

Just as a mirror reflects the image of the one standing in front of it, discovering one's biblical character or persona reflects certain details of a person's life. While it might not be a 100% match in every aspect, it offers a glimpse into who we are, what God has placed inside of us, potential experiences, battles we might face, and strategies we can adopt to secure victory. For example, John the Baptist's biblical character was Elijah, which is why the angel told Zechariah, John's father, that John would come in the spirit and power of Elijah:

But the angel said to him, "Do not be afraid, Zacharias, for your prayer is heard; and your wife Elizabeth will bear you a son, and you shall call his name John. And you will have joy and gladness, and many will rejoice at his birth. For he will be great in the sight of the Lord, and shall drink neither wine nor strong drink. He will also be filled with the Holy Spirit, even from his mother's womb. And he will turn many of the children of Israel to the Lord their God. **He will also go before Him in the spirit and power of Elijah, 'to turn the hearts of the fathers to the children,' and the disobedient to the wisdom of the just, to make ready a people prepared for the Lord." —** *(Luke 1:13-17, NKJV)*

Case Study 1: John the Baptist and Prophet Elijah

Their Greatest Enemy Was the Wife of a Ruling King:
Elijah's greatest enemy was Jezebel, the wife of King Ahab, while John the Baptist's greatest enemy was Herodias. Similarly, Herodias carried a spirit and likeness similar to Jezebel.

Their Enemies Wanted to Capture Them:
Armies were sent three times to capture Elijah, but he responded by calling down fire upon them (2 Kings 1:9-13). John the Baptist was eventually captured and imprisoned (Mark 6:16-17).

Their Enemies Wanted Their Heads:
Jezebel sent a message to Elijah threatening his life, while Herodias requested the head of John the Baptist.
"Then Jezebel sent a messenger to Elijah, saying, 'So let the gods do to me, and more also, if I do not make your life as

the life of one of them by tomorrow about this time.'" — (1 Kings 19:2, NKJV)

"When the daughter of Herodias came in and danced, she pleased Herod and his dinner guests. The king said to the girl, 'Ask me for anything you want, and I'll give it to you.' And he promised her with an oath, 'Whatever you ask I will give you, up to half my kingdom.' She went out and said to her mother, 'What shall I ask for?' 'The head of John the Baptist,' she answered. At once the girl hurried in to the king with the request: 'I want you to give me right now the head of John the Baptist on a platter.' The king was greatly distressed, but because of his oaths and his dinner guests, he did not want to refuse her. So he immediately sent an executioner with orders to bring John's head. The man went, beheaded John in the prison, and brought back his head on a platter. He presented it to the girl, and she gave it to her mother." — (Mark 6:22-28, NKJV)

Case Study 2: Daniel and Joseph

Both Were Captives in a Foreign Land:
Joseph was sold as a slave to Egypt (Genesis 37), while Daniel was taken captive to Babylon (Daniel 1).

God's Favor Was Over Their Lives:
Joseph prospered in everything he did because God was with him. He found favour with Potiphar, the prison warden, and eventually Pharaoh (Genesis 39). Daniel found favour with the steward in charge of their meals, Nebuchadnezzar, for more time to interpret his dream, and King Cyrus (Daniel 1, 2, 6).

Both Had the Gift of Administration:
Joseph managed the affairs of Potiphar and the prison and eventually became the overseer of Egypt under Pharaoh (Genesis 39, 41). Daniel was made ruler over Babylon and chief administrator over all the wise men, later serving as one of the governors under King Darius (Daniel 2:48-49, 6).

Both Interpreted Dreams, Leading to Their Prominence:
Joseph interpreted dreams for the king's cupbearer and baker, and later Pharaoh's, which led to his rise (Genesis 40, 41). Daniel interpreted Nebuchadnezzar's dream, leading to his promotion (Daniel 2).

Both Faced Evil Plots:
Joseph was falsely accused by Potiphar's wife and imprisoned (Genesis 39). Daniel faced an evil plot by other governors, leading to his being thrown into the lion's den (Daniel 6).

Both Were Solution Centers for Kings:
Joseph provided not only the interpretation but also a solution for Pharaoh's dream (Genesis 41). Daniel provided interpretations that were critical for King Nebuchadnezzar, King Belshazzar, and King Darius (Daniel 2, 5, 6).

The Importance of Discovering Your Biblical Character

It's essential to discover and study the life of your biblical character, as this can provide insights into threats, temptations, graces, and mistakes common to both you and your biblical counterpart. For instance, had John the Baptist known and fully understood he came in the spirit and power of Elijah, he might have called down fire when he was captured—similar to Elijah's method of dealing with threats.

Parents and Biblical Characters

Parents should not only seek names for their children from God but also inquire about their biblical character/persona. This can provide deeper insights into their children's identities, enabling parents to guide them with wisdom. Mary, the mother of Jesus, kept the things revealed about Jesus and pondered them in her heart, which is why she could trigger His first miracle at the wedding of Cana (John 2), recognizing His abilities based on what had been revealed to her about Him over the years.

Chapter 5

Discover and Run With Your Vision

"Do you not know that in a race all the runners run [their very best to win], but only one receives the prize? Run [your race] in such a way that you may seize the prize and make it yours!" — (1 Corinthians 9:24, AMP)

There is a race set before each of us, a race with a prize attached to it. When I first encountered the above scripture, I wondered why it said "run your race," given that it also mentions multiple runners. It seemed paradoxical. However, the Holy Spirit provided more insight. Yes, there is a race, but it is not a competitive race against outsiders. Rather, it is a race against our various selves. We all have different versions of ourselves – our **good**, **better**, and **best** selves. How we choose to run this race will determine whether the good, better, or best version of us wins.

What is the Race?

The race set before you is your vision. When God created us, He designed us with a specific vision and purpose that He desires us to discover and pursue. Our birth is purposeful and intentional, and we all have a vision or purpose to fulfill. Our vision is our why, the reason for our creation, and the mission we are ordained to accomplish on earth. What you see will determine your steps and actions and how far you will go. We have a duty to God, ourselves, and others to discover and pursue our God-ordained vision.

"It is God's privilege to conceal things and the king's privilege to discover them." — (Proverbs 25:2, NLT)

Vision is something initially concealed by God and requires us to unravel and discover it. Let's examine how we can discover our vision.

How to Discover Your Vision

Pray and Ask the Holy Spirit

"I will stand at my guard post and station myself on the tower; And I will keep watch to see what He will say to me, and what answer I will give [as His spokesman] when I am reproved. Then the Lord answered me and said, 'Write the vision, and engrave it plainly on [clay] tablets, so that the one who reads it will run.'" — (Habakkuk 2:1-2, AMP)

In the above scripture, Habakkuk mentions standing at his guard post and keeping watch to see what God will say. This involves seeking God's face for clarity concerning our vision. Since the Spirit of God (the Holy Spirit) was present during our creation, He is aware of the vision ordained for us. It requires us to intentionally seek God's face to understand why He created us and what purpose we are destined to fulfill on this earth. You can take time out of your schedule to pray, fast, or even go on a retreat to a place without external distractions to seek God's direction and clarity. The Holy Spirit is the Spirit of truth, able to guide us into the truth about who we are and what God has destined for us since the beginning of time. Once clarity is attained, it is important to write it down—in a journal, tablet, or somewhere you can reference later. This ensures that you don't rely solely on your memory and risk missing out on important details concerning your vision. Discovering and understanding your vision helps you run your race effectively and secure the prize that God has set before you.

Speak with Spiritual Authorities

In some instances, the Holy Spirit can communicate your vision or even confirm it through a human spiritual authority, such as your pastor. If the vision wasn't directly revealed to you, it's important to take the time to seek personal confirmation of that vision and gain further understanding with the help of the Holy Spirit. This is crucial because you are the one who must run with the vision, and gaining a proper understanding is essential for it to propel you forward.

Pay Attention to What Sets You on Fire

Jesus Christ was in the synagogue one day, and He opened the scroll and found the passage where the Prophet Isaiah said:

"The Spirit of the Lord is upon Me (the Messiah), Because He has anointed Me to preach the good news to the poor. He has sent Me to announce release (pardon, forgiveness) to the captives, And recovery of sight to the blind, To set free those who are oppressed (downtrodden, bruised, crushed by tragedy), to proclaim the favorable year of the Lord [the day when salvation and the favor of God abound greatly]."— (Luke 4:18-19, AMP)

This passage resonated deeply with Jesus Christ as He saw it speaking of Himself and His divine mission. The subsequent verses mention that He closed the scroll midway and declared to the congregation in the synagogue that the passage was fulfilled in their hearing that day, through His life.

"Then He rolled up the scroll [having stopped in the middle of the verse], gave it back to the attendant, and sat down [to teach]; and the eyes of all those in the synagogue were [attentively] fixed on Him. He began speaking to them: 'Today this Scripture has been fulfilled in your hearing and in your presence.'"— (Luke 4:20-21, AMP)

Similarly, a passage from the Word of God might jump out to you, revealing a certain aspect of your vision, or a particular issue in the world might ignite your passion, indicating that this issue is aligned with your vision. However, whatever the case might be, verifying this with the Holy Spirit is essential. You can also consult your spiritual authority for clarity and confirmation. By seeking guidance from spiritual authorities and paying attention to what sets your heart on fire, you can gain better clarity on your vision, ensuring that you fully understand it and are prepared to pursue it with determination and passion.

How to Run with Your Vision

Take Action

"Lazy people don't even cook the game they catch, but the diligent make use of everything they find." — (Proverbs 12:27, NLT)

Discovering your vision is important, but taking action to realize that vision is crucial. In the above passage, even catching game during hunting is considered lazy if the game isn't cooked. Hunting represents discovering the vision God has for your life. However, discovery alone is insufficient; what is discovered must be worked on so its value can come to life. Similarly, Habakkuk 2:2 highlights the importance of writing the vision and making it plain so that the one who reads it will run with it:

"Then the LORD answered me and said: 'Write the vision And make it plain on tablets, That he may run who reads it.'" — (Habakkuk 2:2, NKJV)

Writing the vision is great, but interacting with it by identifying and running with the necessary steps for its actualization is key. Your vision is like a newborn baby. While the birth of a child is celebrated, the baby is not left in the hospital; they are nurtured to grow into their full potential. Similarly, treat your vision like a child that needs to be groomed to ensure it becomes everything God has ordained it to be.

Ruth

Naomi's daughter-in-law, Ruth, understood the importance of running with her vision. After her husband's death and their move back to Judah, she decided to care for her mother-in-law and herself. One day, she told Naomi she wanted to go into the fields to glean grains so they wouldn't starve:

"A little sleep, a little slumber, a little folding of the hands to rest— and poverty will come on you like a thief and scarcity like an armed man." — (Proverbs 24:33-34, NIV)

Ruth diligently pursued her new vision. Her hard work was noticed by Boaz and his foreman, who praised her when Boaz inquired about her. Ruth's focus wasn't on finding a husband but on running with her vision. Her hard work and focus, rather than makeup or appearance, caught Boaz's attention. Perhaps she was the only one working in the field when he arrived, which made her stand out. While there's nothing wrong with makeup, the dedication to one's vision is significantly attractive. Little did Ruth know that running with her vision would lead her to work in the fields of her future husband. Being industrious,

Boaz noticed Ruth's tenacity and focus, which contributed to her attractiveness. The rest, as they say, is history.

Focus on Your Vision

Many singles long to find their future spouse. While marriage is beautiful, having your priorities in order is crucial. Run diligently with the vision God has placed in your hands with all your being. While you are doing so, God can align the path of your future spouse with yours. Marriage involves two people running together to achieve a God-ordained vision. Therefore, running diligently with your vision is the starting point for the vision you will pursue in marriage if that is your desire. Run diligently with your vision so the best version of yourself wins. Run to win!

Establish Accountability

Having a vision and running with it is crucial, but there will be times when you get tired. This is where accountability comes in. Having someone you respect to nudge you when you're weary can make all the difference. The Bible underscores this by stating that two are better than one because they can help each other succeed:

"Two people are better off than one, for they can help each other succeed. If one person falls, the other can reach out and help. But someone who falls alone is in real trouble." — (Ecclesiastes 4:9-10, NLT)

No one is an island; we all need others around us to ensure the flames of our vision don't die down. Having a vision buddy system is crucial to provide the extra oil needed, like the five wise virgins, as you run with your vision (Matthew 25:1-13).

Pitfalls To Avoid While Running with Your Vision

Distractions

Life is filled with competing visions, often referred to as distractions. Nehemiah decided to rebuild the wall of Jerusalem, which was in ruins, and he received the support of the king. The people were ready to work, and everything seemed to align until Sanballat, Tobiah, and Geshem showed up:

"But now I said to them, 'You know very well what trouble we are in. Jerusalem lies in ruins, and its gates have been destroyed by fire. Let us rebuild the wall of Jerusalem and end this disgrace!' Then I told them about how the gracious hand of God had been on me, and about my conversation with the king. They replied at once, 'Yes, let's rebuild the wall!' So they began the good work. But when Sanballat, Tobiah, and Geshem the Arab heard of our plan, they scoffed contemptuously. 'What are you doing? Are you rebelling against the king?' they asked. I replied, 'The God of heaven will help us succeed. We, his servants, will start rebuilding this wall. But you have no share, legal right, or historic claim in Jerusalem.'" — (Nehemiah 2:17-20, NLT)

If you read the Book of Nehemiah, you will see the numerous distractions he faced from these agents of distraction, including mental and emotional distractions such as condescending words (Nehemiah 4:1-5), complaints from the people (Nehemiah 5), intimidation (Nehemiah 6), and betrayal from within by a high priest who was colluding with an enemy (Nehemiah 13:4-9, 28). Despite these numerous distractions, Nehemiah remained focused until the wall was built.

In contrast, Amnon, the first son of David, lost focus on his vision of being the next heir to the throne. He became distracted by the idea of sleeping with his half-sister. When he eventually raped her, that distraction cost him his life and halted his vision (2 Samuel 13).

Stay focused on God's vision before you, and don't get distracted.

Discouragement

When pursuing a vision, there are moments when you might question the impact or usefulness of your efforts. This feeling is known as discouragement. Everyone will face discouragement at some point, but it is essential to have systems in place to ensure it doesn't slow you down or bring your vision to a complete halt. Discouragement impedes a person's progress and, if not dealt with, can stop the vision entirely.

Elijah

Elijah was a prophet tasked with restoring the hearts of God's people back to Him, which included destroying the 450 prophets of Baal and the 400 prophets of Asherah:

"And he answered, 'I have not troubled Israel, but you and your father's house have, in that you have forsaken the commandments of the Lord and have followed the Baals. Now therefore, send and gather all Israel to me on Mount Carmel, the four hundred and fifty prophets of Baal, and the four hundred prophets of Asherah, who eat at Jezebel's table.'" — (1 Kings 18:18-19, NKJV)

Elijah had just succeeded in completing the first part of his vision (killing the prophets of Baal) and had not yet embarked on the second half (killing the prophets of Asherah) when discouragement set in. A message from Jezebel filled with demonic words made Elijah, a great prophet, so discouraged that he wanted to die. He became disillusioned and ready to give up until God spoke to him, provided food, and renewed his strength (1 Kings 19).

Discouragement attacks the joy of your vision. The joy of the Lord gives us strength (Nehemiah 8:10) to keep moving forward, and one way to renew this joy is by revisiting the "why" behind the vision God gave you. Remind yourself of the lives being or that will be restored or transformed as a result of your vision. Go over testimonies shared with you, read appreciative notes or text messages from those blessed or inspired by your vision, and speak with vision-minded peers or spiritual authorities for renewed excitement. Remind yourself of the joy that comes to God's heart whenever He sees you partnering with Him in your vision. These systems will help combat any discouragement. Don't lose heart; keep running with your vision, and you will reap your reward in due time.

"Let us not grow weary or become discouraged in doing good, for at the proper time we will reap, if we do not give in." — (Galatians 6:9, AMP)

Rejection

What people don't initially understand is often first rejected. Rejection is not a sign that your vision isn't from God but perhaps an indicator that people don't yet understand it. Jesus Christ was sent to save us from our sins, yet He was misunderstood and rejected by many. This did not stop Him from fulfilling His mission on earth. Keep pressing on, and as people begin to see and accept your vision, it will spread like wildfire and consume all who see and hear about it. The stone initially rejected can become the chief cornerstone if you don't allow rejection to stop you from running with your vision.

"Jesus asked them, 'Have you never read in the Scriptures: "The [very] Stone which the builders rejected and threw away has become the chief Cornerstone; This is the Lord's doing, and it is marvelous and wonderful in our eyes"?'" — (Matthew 21:42, AMP)

Determine in your heart that you will **Run to Win!**

Chapter 6

Build Your Character

Vision Without Character

Vision without character will lead to disaster. A person of character is one who will go far. The foundation of good character is built on the fruit of the Holy Spirit:

"But the fruit of the Spirit is love, joy, peace, longsuffering, kindness, goodness, faithfulness, gentleness, self-control. Against such there is no law." — (Galatians 5:22-23, NKJV)

If you have identified character flaws in your life, it is time to start working on them and building the right character traits. Beauty can get people's attention, but character captures people's hearts:

"Charm can be deceiving, and beauty fades away, but a woman who honours the LORD deserves to be praised." — (Proverbs 31:30, CEV)

Our display of good character honours God because we are ambassadors of God as His children. Let's examine the story of Ruth and Boaz and glean some character traits they exemplified that are crucial to develop during your single season and will be invaluable in your future marriage. This is not an exhaustive list, but includes:

Tenacity

Tenacity, endurance, or diligence is a vital virtue that needs to be built and is often developed through challenges. Ruth was married for ten years before her husband died. The same predicament befell her brother-in-law and father-in-law. She faced multiple burials and immense grief. In those days, a widow could marry her husband's brother, but in Ruth's case, her brother-in-law was also dead. Naomi, her mother-in-law, had also lost her husband, and it was unlikely she would have another son. Despite such tragedy and loss, Ruth remained focused and tenacious. Her tenacity kept her going and led her to pursue a new vision of caring for Naomi and herself by gleaning fields. Her unyielding attitude fueled her excellence while working in Boaz's field, catching the attention of the foreman and Boaz himself.

Sometimes, one might feel weary in doing good, but endurance helps not to give up. Challenges will come, but as my husband says, "We won't back down until we secure victory." This trait must be developed during the single season, as it will be needed in marriage if that is your path. Every marriage will face storms, and it requires building on the right foundation of Jesus and also on the foundation of tenacity/endurance to hold on through the storms:

"Therefore whoever hears these sayings of Mine, and does them, I will liken him to a wise man who built his house on the rock: and the rain descended, the floods came, and the winds blew and beat on that house; and it did not fall, for it was founded on the rock. But everyone who hears these sayings of Mine, and does not do them, will be like a foolish man who built his house on the sand: and the rain descended, the floods came, and the winds blew and beat on that house; and it fell. And great was its fall." — (Matthew 7:24-27, NKJV)

The character displayed by Ruth, to endure and not quit despite challenges, became visible when working in the fields of Boaz and ultimately paved the way for her divine connection to her future spouse. Tenacity or diligence is not restricted to those who want to get married but is a valuable trait to develop for various areas of life, including career, academics, business, ministry, and relationships. There will be times you want to give up, but when such urges come, discipline your mind, spirit, and body to never quit until victory is secured!

Integrity

We are in an age where the virtue of integrity is becoming rare. According to the Cambridge Dictionary, integrity is "the quality of being honest and having strong moral principles that you refuse to change." Integrity means that your yes is yes and your no is no. Boaz exemplified integrity when Ruth approached him on the threshing floor and asked him to cover her, signifying that she wanted to be under his protection as a husband. Instead of quickly eloping with her, Boaz explained that there was another family redeemer ahead of him in line, and he wanted to give that person the opportunity first, respecting the customs of the land despite his love for Ruth.

"And after Boaz had eaten and drunk, and his heart was cheerful, he went to lie down at the end of the heap of grain; and she came softly, uncovered his feet, and lay down. Now it happened at midnight that the man was startled, and turned himself; and there, a woman was lying at his feet. And he said, 'Who are you?' So she answered, 'I am Ruth, your maidservant. Take your maidservant under your wing, for you are a close relative.' Then he said, 'Blessed are you of the Lord, my daughter! For you have shown more kindness at the end than at the beginning, in that you did not go after young men, whether poor or rich. And now, my daughter, do not fear. I will do for you all that you request, for all the people of my town know that you are a virtuous woman. Now it is true that I am a close relative; however, there is a relative closer than I. Stay this night, and in the morning it shall be that if he will

perform the duty of a close relative for you—good; let him do it. But if he does not want to perform the duty for you, then I will perform the duty for you, as the Lord lives! Lie down until morning.'" — (Ruth 3:7-13, NKJV)

When our integrity is built on the Word of God, it produces a solid believer who is immovable, regardless of the challenges or temptations they may face. Integrity builds a foundation of trust in any relationship, be it romantic, career, or platonic.

Kindness

Whatever you sow, you will reap. Kindness was a virtue deeply embedded in Ruth, and she reaped kindness from others, including the foreman, Boaz, and Naomi. Her reputation for kindness preceded her, and it was one of the traits Boaz highlighted when speaking with her.

"Boaz went over and said to Ruth, 'Listen, my daughter. Stay right here with us when you gather grain; don't go to any other fields. Stay right behind the young women working in my field. See which part of the field they are harvesting, and then follow them. I have warned the young men not to treat you roughly. And when you are thirsty, help yourself to the water they have drawn from the well.' Ruth fell at his feet and thanked him warmly. 'What have I done to deserve such kindness?' she asked. 'I am only a foreigner.' 'Yes, I know,' Boaz replied. 'But I also know about everything you have done for your mother-in-law since the death of your husband. I have heard how you left your father and mother

and your own land to live here among complete strangers. May the Lord, the God of Israel, under whose wings you have come to take refuge, reward you fully for what you have done.' 'I hope I continue to please you, sir,' she replied. 'You have comforted me by speaking so kindly to me, even though I am not one of your workers.' At mealtime Boaz called to her, 'Come over here, and help yourself to some food. You can dip your bread in the sour wine.' So she sat with his harvesters, and Boaz gave her some roasted grain to eat. She ate all she wanted and still had some left over." — (Ruth 2:8-14, NLT)

Developing the virtue of kindness is crucial, as you never know whom you will meet. Rebekah's kindness to a stranger (Abraham's servant) at the well was the virtue he hoped to see in the bride-to-be for Isaac (Genesis 24). Little did she know that her act of kindness would pave the way for her future. We are often just a few people away from the answer we need, and kindness is a virtue that can connect us with our destiny connectors and destiny helpers. Be kind!

Remain Submitted and Under Authority

Submission is the willingness to be under the authority of the Word, the Holy Spirit, and human authorities in one's life. It stems from a heart posture of humility, indicating a readiness to be corrected, directed, and guided by sources outside oneself. These sources include the Word of God, the Holy Spirit, and human spiritual authorities. This is crucial because everyone is led by something or someone, and whoever leads us will determine the fruits we produce. Submission applies to both men and women alike.

Examples of Submission in Scripture

Boaz was a man of God and was under the authority of the principles of God and the customs of his kinsmen, which is why he showed integrity in first speaking with the first family redeemer of Ruth before making his move to marry her. Jesus Christ, though single and even though He was the Son of God, He was under the authority of His parents, and we can see that displayed when He yielded to His mother's nudge to convert water to wine at the wedding in Cana (John 2:1-11). Ruth was a woman under the authority of Naomi, and when Naomi provided her instructions on what to do, she might not have even understood why she was doing so, but she followed the instructions (Ruth 3:1-9).

"Who are you?" he asked. "I am your servant Ruth," she replied. "Spread the corner of your covering over me, for you are my family redeemer." — (Ruth 3:9, NLT)

The Importance of Submission

Ruth's readiness to be under Boaz's authority and covering stemmed from her practice of submission long before marriage. Remember, the single season is a season of preparation and training. By submitting to the authority in our lives—whether it's the Word of God, the Holy Spirit, or human spiritual authorities—we set the foundation for future responsibilities and relationships.

In conclusion, submission is crucial for both men and women. It ensures that we are led by divine forces that produce good fruit in our lives. By embracing submission, we honour God and align ourselves with His divine order, paving the way for a fruitful and fulfilling journey.

Chapter 7

Visualize Your Desired Future

Visualize Your Future

In his book *The 7 Habits of Highly Effective People: Powerful Lessons in Personal Change*, Stephen Covey said, "We create twice; first in our minds and then in reality." During your single season, it is important to visualize the kind of future you desire and begin to take steps toward it. Ask yourself, "What kind of future do I want? What kind of future relationships (romantic and/or platonic) do I desire? What kind of home or family do I want?" It's time to visualize your future!

When I was single, I had heard numerous stories, both true and fictional, about the friction between wives and mothers-in-law. I recall a senior girl in high school telling me she wanted her mother-in-law to be deceased before she married. This didn't sit right with me, and I believed this didn't have to be the case. When I encountered the relationship between Ruth and Naomi (her mother-in-law) in the Bible and saw the love, respect, and intimacy in their relationship, I realized it was possible to have a fabulous relationship with my mother-in-law as well. Their genuine relationship showed me that a positive connection is achievable, as Ruth's kindness to Naomi continued even after her husband's death.

"Then Naomi heard in Moab that the Lord had blessed his people in Judah by giving them good crops again. So Naomi and her daughters-in-law got ready to leave Moab to return to her homeland. With her two daughters-in-law she set out from the place where she had been living, and they took the road that would lead them back to Judah. But on the way, Naomi said to her two daughters-in-law, 'Go back to your mothers' homes. And may the Lord reward you for your kindness to your husbands and to me. May the Lord bless you with the security of another marriage.' Then she kissed them good-bye, and they all broke down and wept. 'No,' they said. 'We want to go with you to your people.' But Naomi replied, 'Why should you go on with me? Can I still give birth to other sons who could grow up to be your husbands? No, my daughters, return to your parents' homes, for I am too old to marry again. And even if it were possible, and I were to get married tonight and bear sons, then what? Would you wait for them to grow up and refuse to marry someone else? No, of course not, my daughters! Things are far more bitter for me than for you because the Lord himself has raised his fist against me.' And again they wept together, and Orpah kissed her mother-in-law good-bye. But Ruth clung tightly to Naomi. 'Look,' Naomi said to her, 'your sister-in-law has gone back to her people and to her gods. You should do the same.' But Ruth replied, 'Don't ask me to leave you and turn

back. Wherever you go, I will go; wherever you live, I will live. Your people will be my people, and your God will be my God. Wherever you die, I will die, and there I will be buried. May the Lord punish me severely if I allow anything but death to separate us!' When Naomi saw that Ruth was determined to go with her, she said nothing more. So the two of them continued on their journey. When they came to Bethlehem, the entire town was excited by their arrival. 'Is it really Naomi?' the women asked. 'Don't call me Naomi,' she responded. 'Instead, call me Mara, for the Almighty has made life very bitter for me. I went away full, but the Lord has brought me home empty. Why call me Naomi when the Lord has caused me to suffer and the Almighty has sent such tragedy upon me?' So Naomi returned from Moab, accompanied by her daughter-in-law Ruth, the young Moabite woman. They arrived in Bethlehem in late spring, at the beginning of the barley harvest." — (Ruth 1:6-22, NLT)

Encountering this story assured me it was possible. I began to visualize such a future with my mother-in-law, even though I wasn't in a relationship at the time. To God's glory, what started as a visual picture in my mind became a reality.

Ask yourself: "What kind of future do I want? What kind of future relationships (romantic and/or platonic) do I desire? What kind of home or family do I want?" It's time to visualize your future!

Epilogue

Every season of your life has been intentionally orchestrated and designed by God for you to live a rich and fulfilling life. This race of life is not a sprint but a marathon, filled with different seasons to navigate and enjoy before moving on to the next.

Marriage is a beautiful season, but to truly enjoy it, you must first embrace and maximize your single season which precedes it. Your single season is not a mistake but an essential, vibrant time waiting for you to engage with and discover its hidden treasures.

As you embrace this single season, take along the Holy Spirit, the perfect tour guide for your singlehood, and embark on this journey with confidence, patience, expectation, and a sense of adventure! Ride this season with joy, knowing you will discover, become, and reflect everything God has perfectly crafted for you in this season.

Enjoy the ride!

A Sinner's Prayer

I will be delighted to lead you in receiving Jesus Christ as your personal Lord and Saviour. If you would like to take this fabulous step today, please say this prayer with me:

"Lord Jesus Christ, I believe you are the Son of God and I believe You died for me on the cross of Calvary. I know I am a sinner and today, I come to You to forgive me of all my sins and to make me a brand new creation. I accept You as my personal Lord and Saviour. Thank you Jesus for forgiving me and make me born again, in Jesus' name, amen"

Name and Signature: _____

Date: _____

Congratulations! You are now born- again! This means you have been engrafted into the kingdom and family of Jesus Christ. Truly, your life will not remain the same. If you made this decision today, I would love to hear from you and provide resources for your new journey! Please kindly visit www.cccghq.org/saved or share your testimony with me at ibukun.adewusi@cccghq.org

Contact the Author

Thank you for taking the time to read this book. I'm positive you were blessed by it. I would be delighted to hear your testimonies on its impact on your life and those around you.

You can stay connected with me through the following platforms:

Instagram: ibukun.adewusi | **Youtube:** Ibukun Adewusi
Email: ibukun.adewusi@cccghq.org

Support the Author

Review the Book

About the Author

Ibukun Adewusi, alongside her husband, Emmanuel Adewusi are the founding and lead pastors of Cornerstone Christian Church of God. Together, they have been called to "bring restoration and transformation to all by teaching, preaching and demonstrating the gospel of Jesus Christ".

She adores the mandate she has received to 'bring restoration and transformation to nations by rescuing and preserving families'. Through her book, '*Synergy: The Essence of Marriage*', and her video series '*Loveseat with Pastor Ibukun*', she aspires to see families blossom, flourish, & fulfill the vision God intended for them since the beginning of creation.

Ibukun Adewusi is joyfully married to Emmanuel Adewusi, her lovely husband. Together, they are building a thriving Christ-centered family.

Additional References

Books

Boelcke, George J. *Colorful Personalities: Discover Your Personality Type Through the Power of Colors.* Vantage Publishing, 2009.

Chapman, Gary. *The 5 Love Languages: Secrets to Love That Lasts.* The Northfield Publishing, 2009.

Covey, Stephen R. *The 7 Habits of Highly Effective People: Powerful Lessons in Personal Change.* Free Press, 2004.

Articles and Encyclopedias

Britannica, The Editors of Encyclopaedia. "Rowan Atkinson." *Encyclopedia Britannica*, 2 May 2024, https://www.britannica.com/biography/Rowan-Atkinson.

Websites

Cambridge Dictionary. "Integrity." Cambridge University Press, https://dictionary.cambridge.org/dictionary/english/integrity.

Cambridge Dictionary. "Single Someone/Something Out." Cambridge University Press, https://dictionary.cambridge.org/dictionary/english/single-out.

Missouri Department of Elementary and Secondary Education. "Trauma-Informed Care." Retrieved from https://earlyconnections.mo.gov/professionals/trauma-informed-care.

Mountainside Treatment Center. "Fight, Flight, Freeze, Fawn: Our Natural Response to Threats." Retrieved from https://mountainside.com/blog/mental-health/fight-flight-freeze-fawn-our-natural-response-to-threats.

Videos

Cornerstone Christian Church of God. "Overcoming Trauma." YouTube, https://youtu.be/haOqcU0gT2o?si=JOWuYCwGfTuu4ut_.

Trading Coach UK. "Inside Rolls Royce- Documentary." YouTube, Premiered March 5, 2019, https://www.youtube.com/watch?v=pndoAjymnMM.

Reports

American Psychological Association. "Trauma." 2008, Retrieved from

https://www.apa.org/topics/trauma#:~:text=Trauma%20is%20an%20emotional%20response,symptoms%20like%20headaches%20or%20nausea.

www.ingramcontent.com/pod-product-compliance
Lightning Source LLC
Chambersburg PA
CBHW050250010526
44107CB00003B/258